T0150667

DANCING UNDER A BLOODLESS MOON

Winner of the International Beverly Prize 2018

The Judge's Citation:
'This is a superb collection of impeccably crafted poems.
Hale writes of a world of journeys, in haunting lines that are both
melodic and powerfully concrete. I don't think there is a bad line in the
entire book. I don't think there is a bad poem in the entire book.
This is a classic collection that draws the reader in, and that
leaves a ghostly and almost ethereal afterglow not only
with each poem but with the collection as a whole.
This is a work of high distinction and incredible artistry.'
– DR BRUCE MEYER, *critic and poet*

David Hale

Dancing Under
A Bloodless Moon

Winner of the International Beverly Prize 2018

First published in 2020
by The Black Spring Press Group
Suite 333, 19-21 Crawford Street
Marylebone, London w1H 1PJ
United Kingdom

Cover design and typeset by Edwin Smet

All rights reserved
© 2020 David Hale

The right of David Hale to be identified as author of
this work has been asserted in accordance with section 77
of the Copyright, Designs and Patents Act 1988

ISBN 978-1-913606-15-2

WWW.EYEWEARPUBLISHING.COM

For Don

Born in Prestwick, Ayrshire, David Hale has lived in Greece, London, Oxfordshire, Kent and Bristol, but now divides his time between Cornwall and Gloucestershire. His first pamphlet *The Last Walking Stick Factory* was published in 2011 by *Happenstance*; his second, *In Bedlam's Wood*, won Templar's pamphlet competition. He has had work published in a range of magazines and anthologies, most recently in *Gutter, The High Window* and *The North*. He teaches refugees and asylum seekers English in Gloucester, and grows vegetables for a retreat centre near Stroud. He also looks after a couple of welsh cobs on a part time basis. *Dancing Under a Bloodless Moon* is his first full collection, and won Eyewear's Beverly Prize in 2018.

TABLE OF CONTENTS

MEMORY

The train from Schipol is a seam of light
travelling through the dusk
between snow-edged field, embankment.

Father is drinking coffee, mother holding my hand
when a man appears, dark-bearded, smiling.
He holds out a gold coin, says, *Take it, it's for you.*

I look up at father, at mother's pale face,
down at the coin – how light it is, this flat gold moon –
barely notice as the man disappears.

The train crosses into Germany
and father peels away the gold. Beneath is
chocolate. I bite into it, wondering at such alchemy.

So where there is gold, there's chocolate –
something learned on this bright holiday train.
From now on, no coin is safe from my jaws:

base metal is scraped, bitten, causing pain,
confusion, till the penny drops, so to speak.
You could say I remember this. But I don't.

I am painting from memory, and someone else
is moving my hand.

WOJTEK

i.m. AJH

I like to imagine you
stumbling across the parade
the day the Polish army
marched through Glasgow
in September forty-six:
slim, dark, stethoscope in hand,
a little hung-over,
not exactly cheering
as they pass down the Broomielaw
to the music of pipe and drum,
but struck by the sight
of a brown bear shambling
along in the ranks: waving,
cavorting, catching cigarettes
thrown by the crowd.
This is where I lose sight of you —
heading on towards
the Infirmary, disappearing
through the doors
of the dissection room,
where you chuckle
over its ursine antics
as you slice up the body
laid out on your slab.

DEER, MIDSUMMER

Pursued by moon-teeth before meadow-cut
she falls onto a bed of foxtail, plantain,
red fescue, blood and saliva streaking
her crushed throat. Left to die, she drags
herself through hawkweed, sweet-cicely,
rye, towards the shores of that other world.
I find her hyperventilating in the heat
but with no blade or bullet to effect
a swift transition, only a length of field-maple
solid enough to snap her outstretched neck.
She doesn't scream or look me in the eye,
but beyond to cloud-shadow and bleary sky;
she doesn't curse me for what I have to do.
A prayer of honey-bees and scarlet beetles
mark her passing. How quickly the meadow's
dark mouth fastens to her bloody neck
as I loop baler-twine around one shapely leg –
one beautiful black hoof, draw her through
campion and vetch to this resting place,
to be covered with sprays of wych-elm,
and wild-apple from where she'll come to me
in dream, and press hot wet lips to my cheek
as if in absolution.

ON FIREWORKS NIGHT

When you refuse to drop the chip-wrapper filched
from behind the bandstand, I realize
for all your speed and indifference to the crackle
of what sounds like small-arms fire,

unlike your illustrious lurcher forebears
you lack the discipline needed to be a messenger dog,
dodging bullets as you race back from some
outlying trench; and suspect that any message

secreted in your collar would in all probability
be obliterated when wading through mud,
or torn when ducking under wire that, nicking
your shaggy unmilitary neck, would have you

yelping like a hell-hound as you dart in past a battery
and playing hard to get with your handler,
in all probability an earlier version of myself,
who would prefer to be cowering

in the depths of some dug-out and not chasing you
round in circles, until tempted into a bunker
by a mess-tin of bully-beef, you're persuaded
to part with your urgent dispatch.

CORBIERE'S SOW

The hours of darkness
spent dancing under a bloodless moon,

here he is at 8am in evening dress
in the courtyard of a cheap hotel,

humming to himself as he paints
a pair of eyes on his forehead,

peers into the mirror and smudges
each absinthe-green pupil to better effect.

A songbird sings in an upstairs window,
a servant smiles then shakes his head,

a little boy stares at the sow decked out
in red and blue ribbons that breakfasts

on last night's slops. Satisfied, the poet
declaims a line or two of Nerval,

dons a stolen mitre, whistles his pig to heel
and strolls down to the Spanish Steps,

ready for a world that's not quite
ready for him this warm spring morning.

THE TRIALS OF KAUNOS

(Part two)

The first, heat,
   the second a blue boat
bucking through
   river traffic, the third,
Scylla and Charybdis
   of the orange trees –
pancake, pistachios,
   much screeching;
the fourth, heat,
   the fifth, past cypress,
cemetery, an old man
   under a lemon tree –
yellow pears, honey,
   fermenting pomegranate
juice – but lacking
   a shadow; the sixth,
heat, the seventh,
   head-scarfed, soft
words – peach, apricot,
   a pool of stillness –
tempting, but, no;
   the eighth, an ogre
asleep on a divan
   between river and flame-
filled orchard, her familiar
   inexperienced – plums,
baklava on a painted box
   but many wasps –
no shade; the ninth,
   heat.

HEY, MAYAKOVSKY

After Rodchenko

You're making me uneasy:
what have I done to deserve such a look?

is it my lack of political commitment –
the limp bourgeois images that leak from my pen?

Or perhaps it's not me you're looking at
but some guy with a scythe

who wants to put you out of your misery
before the next round of show-trials begin.

Forget about him. Tell me something
about the self-indulgent lyric,

or why the revolution went sour;
how it feels to be standing in Rodchenko's studio

listening to a blackbird sing as spring's
lungs expand in the Moscow dusk.

KYRIL'S TALE

Is it true? they ask as he limps back from the bog,
gobs into a steel spittoon, settles in his seat by the stove.

True? Of course it's true, true as the boils on my mother's arse:
buy me one and I'll tell you the story.

One autumn, we're in Poznań awaiting the visit of a Party Boss
whose staff have declared wants to shoot a bear,

the comrades to arrange it. A bear, he growls,
the bastard wanted to shoot one of our bears.

So after much vodka, some bright spark who still
had the power of speech says let's commandeer a circus bear

install it in a hut deep in the forest. A circus bear, he grunts,
sinking his slivovitz – problem sorted.

When said bigshot arrives, all epaulettes and entourage
of apparatchik arse-lickers,

says if things go well, a new house, a car, that sort of thing,
he's told we hunt at dawn.

So we're out in the birch woods freezing our bollocks off,
tracking this poor old bear

turfed out of his hut for the sake of diplomatic relations,
who's running through the trees,

bewildered by our shouts, bullets whistling past his snout,
finally we catch sight of him

standing on the far side of a clearing
watching some old guy cycling up a forest track.

Of course that bear knows all about bicycles.
Next thing we know he's haring after the old guy,

who leaps off his bike, the bear leaps on,
builds up a head of steam and cycles off through the trees

leaving us in stunned silence –
wondering if we're about to head east for a nice little holiday.

But no. The big man laughs so hard he nearly wets himself.
And we join in. The rest's a blur,

but later, before passing out in the bog at the Pravoskaya,
I remember worrying about that bear,

if his wild kin would accept him
once the smell of greasepaint faded from his fur.

There you have it, he growls and smacks his hand on the table –
a tale from the good old days.

THE GIFT

To receive a gift is to be honoured:
shark's teeth, silver drachma, single malts.
I've received my share from those I've taught,
each a puzzle to be unpicked, a statement
or response to a set of signposts through the maze.

So a small spherical piece of camel dung
from the slopes of Mount Sinai – concise yet cryptic;
what could I do but cup it in my palm
note its tint and texture – a little grainy,
the colour of good shit – and lift it to my nose.

One waft to a wild beast would determine
its host's sex, age and state of health –
from which pilgrim track it came,
one of a string laden with panniers
picking its way up over rock and sand.

But as I am not, instead receive such
skewed images as the scraps in the dark
cupboard labelled 'desert and camel' allow,
and tend towards interpretation,
as if the entrails of the beast lay before me.

Were we talking skincare, the merits of recycling,
or was this a comment on the way I look
at 5 to 9 each Thursday morning?
In the face of such generosity,
I wonder what I might give in return?

LAMENT FOR A CAR SALESMAN

Eugene sells cars in
a palace of chrome and glass,
a goldfish bowl of
absolute transparency
that has nothing if not class.

Attractive, you'd think
to one who worked his way up
selling heaps of scrap –
wears his service-history
on his sleeve – no t-cut or

touching up will hide
the scars on his bodywork.
Yes, it pays the bills.
But he hates this sterile place,
feels constrained in its airless

showroom that aspires
to art, reduced to test drives
around the block
in machines that clock every
due statistic of mileage

done and engine hum,
have aerodynamics the
envy of a bat –
with no opportunity
to throw a punch, or flog a

motor over lunch,
make some punter feel it's his
lucky day, until
halfway back to Haringey
the head-gasket aerates his

bonnet. No. And how
he hates the gratitude in
their eyes, those asides,
such a straight bloke Eugene, as
they sign on the dotted line.

As for the meetings...
Sometimes he wakes before dawn –
wants to scream: sod the
quotas, the annual trip to
Minnesota. You've got to

get out Eugene – you've
got to leave these drones with their
air-con dreams behind,
head for the wide open road
while you still have time.

THE BARRIER

There is no such thing as society
— Margaret Thatcher

Tennants in hand,
he turns up at the Community Centre
grunts, nods, gobs into a gutter
choked with carry-out
and crumpled fag packets.

The ambulance looks forlorn.
He grimaces when I ask him to clean it,
check the oil and tyres,
and see if its fuel has mysteriously
evaporated overnight.

At the lights he rolls one,
with the first sign of animation
urges me to let the hand-brake off,
to ram the Merc in front —
words come out of his broken mouth

as if broken themselves.
Slumped against the glass —
I give him one of my looks,
and wonder where he was last night,
if the project's doing him any good.

At the Day-Centre he slips away.
I round up the old folks
who squabble over seats, swap insults,
ignore me till he reappears
thumbing his nose, full of sudden purpose.

By the foot of Camden Place
he's settled them, is laughing
at their tasteless jokes and tales of woe
as I inch through traffic
cut up by taxis, buses, white vans.

At the Barrier,
they follow him into the lift.
The smell is intense. Stray fingers
fondle my buttocks through the crush.
I'm trapped until the doors open

and he shepherds them
into the visitor centre,
indicates the surge of the river seaward
with a majestic sweep
of his tracked and scrawny arm.

MUGS

After Gwen Harwood

Handed a filthy mug of tea
that first morning in the forest shelter,
how they laughed at my discomfort,
said a bit of dirt's no bad thing for the guts,
as tea stewed on the stove.

It took days to get used to drinking
out of cracked, unhygienic vessels,
to the habit of dumping them on bench and wood-pile,
or in the rat-infested larder
until they became impromptu petri-dishes,

fostering all manner of pale grey,
green and often furry organisms,
or functioned as nesting-boxes
for a range of curious small-fry.
After a week or two, unwilling

to be seen as too refined in my tastes,
I too was leaving them to the mercy
of the elements, only took time
to wash them on days when it was
too wet or cold to work outside.

Periodically, even the most hard-core
members of the team would revolt
against the onset of ooze and grime.
There'd be a cull, the most offensive
being re-deployed for target practice,

or as containers for spent chainsaw oil.
One morning, we'd jump into
the battered pick-up, bump down
to the charity shop and sort through
a selection of mugs seen as surplus

to requirements by discerning residents
of the town, and come away with a box
of pristine mugs, that in a few months
would sink to a level of degradation
that would shock even us.

COMPOSITION BY STEALTH

WH Davies Lambeth 1899

The library shut, you limp back to the Ark
sit in a Windsor chair in a dark corner
of the cavernous kitchen where men gather –
mad Horace with his withered garlands,
Flanagan rambling on about being king of Mayo –
and other less friendly souls. After eating,
an idea forming, you ignore the clatter
of pans, the abuse and drunken words,
close your eyes and retreat into a place
of clean rhythms and short rhymes, arrange
words on the blank page of your mind,
sounding them out silently, beat by beat
until the poem's assembled like the chair
you're sitting in – stretcher, comb, spindle,
each line fitting snugly into the next,
committed to memory, until there's time
and space away from suspicious eyes
in this over-crowded hostel that reeks
of cabbage, liquor and wasted lives –
to note it down on a discarded handbill,
to hide it in a hat brim, the lining of your coat.

REJECTION

There is no time to stand and stare

Footsore, a solitary penny in your pocket,
you stump back to the hostel in Churchyard Row.
Without glancing at the sheaf of poems
you shove handfuls into the wood-stove
and brood as the ashes of your invention
sail up the chimney, out into the sooty air.
Consumed with rage at editors, printers,
the poor sods you tried to sell verse to,
you smack your head into the chimney-piece
again and again, unable to see how far
and wide your work's being disseminated,
how many eyes can see your charred rhymes
settle on ledge, roof-tile and gull-wing,
on the margins of that blank autumn day.

IS IT THE WOODPECKER

Or two blackbirds battering
    each other on the bank
that sets you off as we descend
    into the wooded valley –
a rush of words – your first
    that morning – spoken
to no one in particular.
    After the pub, his fists,
matter of fact, somehow
    detached, but felt
in the shift of body memory.
    You lapse into silence
as we head up a sunlit side-valley –
    birdsong and wild garlic –
looser, posture more erect,
    as if motion eases
anger cogged inside.
    We pass tangled ash-thickets
reach the ice-bound lake,
    you're no longer whispering
I'll kill him when I find him –
    but picking up rocks and broken
branches – whooping with glee
    as they shatter its surface –
streams of bubbles released
    from its chill depths.

TIMES

With five minutes of silence left
the room heavy with the scent
of lemon geraniums,

he watches from the depths
of his crumpled anorak
as the paper crosshatches
with calculations:

      244,

7,420,

           178,000.
Sliding to the seat's edge
he grins, suddenly intoxicated
by such wealth of number:
months, days, hours, life
reduced to multiples of time.

Jaw unclenching,
he is lifted from inwardness
those few moments,

oblivious to the old Mill's
warren of voices.

But beyond seconds the rush fades.
He wants more,
but I am unprepared
to enter the realm of microseconds.

MONDAY 29TH JULY 1822

After 3 days of squalls from NW

The house full of the cries of sickly children,
he pins paper to the lid of his paint-box

heads past the old pleasure gardens and
shielding his eyes against the glare of a sky

less turbulent than in recent days,
sketches cloudscapes that refuse to stay still

or conform to the principles of slow
picturesque composition – lost

in the timelessness of process until purblind
and out of ochre, he sees that to truly

understand the moods and vagaries of
these shifting vapours, this source of light

through which all vision is granted,
he must paint it again and again and again

THE PEST HOUSE

So poor a soldier did Coleridge prove to be,
he was detailed to nurse a comrade with typhus
in the grounds of the Henley work-house.

Worn out after six nights
sitting by the narrow workhouse cot –
mopping his comrade's brow
soothing him with story and song,
by the seventh he seems to hover
some seconds over the sick-bed
before falling forward into dream
in which a sheaf of unopened letters
bursts into violet and blue flames
and illuminates a ring of stern
disapproving faces that whisper
of debt, debauchery, dead siblings –
among them his father who tries
to say something through the side
of his strange and frozen mouth –
words that when they finally come
are like body-blows that leave him
lying on the cold stone flags,
until he's woken by cries of water,
for god's sake water, by a lack
of flame flickering in the grate.

THE PACK

Caged behind the barn,
they sleep in the heavy darkness
of the fern-filled clough,
until some sound
real or imagined,
in or out of dream
sets them off –
the valley is filled
with the music
of a pack in full tongue,
the trick of the fells
making the sound
almost unnatural,
a haunting echo and delay
that filters through
to that territory between
sleep and waking,
where I find myself
running through bracken,
unsure if I'm asleep
or awake, man or beast,
but knowing I must escape
the jaws that pursue me
in and out of moonlight
all through the summer night.

TWO DOGS

How busy this kitchen is.
Yet unobserved,
a little grey dog has snuck in
behind the wan-looking woman
with an infant on her lap.

How like a dog to find a quiet place
to dream the day away –
how comfortable he looks
curled in the crib – how cross she'll be
when she finds him there.

Until then, he's oblivious
to the man in black bearing gifts
for the new babe,
the couple churning butter –
to words, movement, everything

but a deep and satisfyingly doggy sleep
full of rabbits, sheep-dung
and choice things to eat.
Unlike his fellow, a pale hunting dog
who looks on hungrily

as a man in a felt hat raises
a bowl of milk to his lips –
who waits patiently for all these
sturdy Flemish peasants
to rush out into the cool autumn morning

to cry *stop thief*, or *fire* —
so he can make off
with a half-moon of cheese,
the cold cut laid on a blue plate,
the soft white loaf that lies beside it.

FRANK MANSELL'S PLAN

Disgusted by the team's performance that summer
he sits each of the lads down in the snug,
quizzes them about their time and place of birth
details some are distinctly hazy about.
Through long winter evenings by the stove
he plots their astrological charts and works out
the perfect position for each of them
by signs gifted by the moon and turning earth:
Sagittarius for pacemen, Taurus for openers,
Capricorn the keeper. So when nets begin,
frost still scorching the fringes of the outfield,
he allocates these new roles, overcomes any muttering
about playing out of their comfort zones.
By the time swallows flock over the beacon,
thanks to the influence of key celestial bodies,
the team has won every match it's played.

AN ASH

Rooted close to the upper wall of Park Wood
in the soak of a field-spring,
that seeps downhill through the rut
and hummock of hoof churn,

it was storm-felled millennium time,
taken by a southerly, the weight
of the wind after weeks of rain,
lay weather-darkened until trimmed
and sectioned, dragged from the bog,

it was planked-up one spring morning,
stacked in the woodshed
to season and breathe,
to pass through that mysterious shift
from one state to the next.

From where, some months on,
it began to disperse: to St Neots as a stool,
Stourbridge as a Windsor chair,
the village school for playground benches,
each piece worked by different hands

this last plank into a table-top by me,
its lower edge soft, fluffy with rot,
spoke-shaved, sanded down through the grades,
oiled to bring out the grain's salmon paleness,
its ripples and dark swirls.

REGRET

One bright morning I took a bowsaw
to my neighbour's birch believing
it cast shadows across my waking hours,
unaware of the volume of sap
that surged through its pale boughs.

Alarmed this towering tree
could bleed so vigorously,
I stowed my saw and wished for wind,
rain, mist, darkness – anything
to hide the sight of its seeping limbs.

All afternoon it dripped and on into night,
each drip amplified in dream, each
stump distorted by the lens of sleep.

NINETEEN-SEVENTY-SEVEN

we drive through the summer night
fuelled by sulphate and petrol
siphoned from parked cars
i don't know what to do with my life
or that you will soon lose yours
but i do know we're about sixty-six miles
south of reality and will be lucky
to make it home before dawn
and i don't know why i'm so drawn to you
why when we touch i can barely
see the road ahead, but i do know
i've got to get out of this shitty little town
and need cash to do so gardening
for old mrs c who's drinking
because pumpkin's a goner
and the whole world's going to hell

ACCORDION CRIME

It sat proud in the police auction,
amidst the stuffed parrots,
suit-cases, carpets and whisks,

a real piece of craftsmanship
with its inlay, fretwork
and bakelite strips.

Lifted from the premises
of some ageing tunesmith
who'd failed to drop the latch

on his way back from the Duke,
it ended up in the monthly sale:
scuffed, a little worse for wear,

a couple of keys gapped
like old teeth, but wheezing still,
dreaming of foxtrot and tango,

a pearl amongst swine;
even though I'd never played one,
thirty quid, and it was mine.

AT THE SIGN OF THE WHITE HORSE

Shakespeare's sonnets were set by two compositors,
one of whom was prone to making mistakes.

The lane full of fellow printers heading
for the stews and alehouses of Southwark,
how irritated you are at being stuck
in a darkened pressroom with seven more
sonnets to set, because the journeyman
has the sweats and master's distracted
by a writ served late last evening leaving
you to deal with a rush and tangle of words
beneath the ill humours of a sick moon
and the reek of Fleet Ditch, with no help
from the pox-ridden excuse of an apprentice
who stokes your anger at pleasure delayed,
at having to reset these ragged proofs
that blur before tired and bloodshot eyes.

LATE SUMMER

Walking the orchard
this still moonlit night,
dog before me
working the perimeters
of shadowy vision,
I climb over the wall
and see our mare
standing motionless
by the fence,
having heard my tread,
what I took to be stealth
and near silence.
I know why she's there.
Scenting an apple,
or maybe two
of the spiked windfalls
she so craves,
she paws at the fence
as I cross the field,
and whickering
ever more urgently,
takes slice after slice
from my palm, pips
and juice dripping
from her great soft mouth
as she pulps them,
all the while staring off
into the distance
at something I just can't see.

FRIEDA

I'm stirring white sauce when she rings
to say that Bobby's disappeared –
search parties sent out, sheds checked –
how worried she is.

As the mixture thickens, I know
the whole road will be rejoicing; someone
may have helped him on his way,
the river conveniently close and deep.

I try not to feel irritated as she goes on
about new gates, holes in the fence,
Bobby's dear little face – how at eighty-nine,
she can't have another one, then rings off.

The sauce begins its slow volcanic bubble.
And I imagine her alone in her riverside room,
smoking, fretting, sipping gin, the weight
of his coat and cruel paws dragging her down.

SCENT

I'm driving home
on a dirty morning
in late December

wind and drizzle,
the dark canvas
of a downland road,

when from over the brow
a line of men appear,
dogs in tow.

Even at a distance
there's something
about their gait,

closer still,
about the coiled energy
of the dogs' backs,

grizzled lurchers
decoding the scent
of ditch and bank.

They scatter at the last
possible moment,
but it's not till I pass

the slew of vans
across the verge
that it comes to me —

out for sport,
it's hares they're after,
but anything will do.

AXEHEAD

The moment I touch its ice-cold cheek
I know what to do. Picking out a piece

of straight-grained ash, I bring strength
to its neck, a natural curve to belly and heel,

make it limber and tough, a perfect haft
to be hammered into the sleeping head.

When finished, weighing and hefting it,
I see you Father for the first time in years,

out by the barn, hewing your way through
a pile of logs, shadowy figures beyond –

it's my turn to feel the shudder of impact,
to lay this axe-head under the bed

to bless my off-spring with the sharpness
that's seen us through since all this started.

INTENSIVE CARE

For Don

Wired up and awash with morphine,
you're close to melting point
when Buster slips in through the ward doors
licks your hand before settling down
to his decades-old ritual
of dispatching can after can of dogfood,
the pert line of cylindrical moulds
which someone has kindly emptied out
onto the scuffed and glowing floor;
unperturbed by the bleep of machines,
passing nurses who absentmindedly
stop to stroke a soft and shaggy ear –
the howls of encouragement
coming from the circle of shadowy
but deeply familiar faces
invited in to observe this spectacle –
one who turns and waves
his hand fanning out like a peacock's tail;
even though in the smoking embers
of your mind you know the dog is dead
as you may be in half an hour,
you suspect this event will go viral,
showcasing as it does a level
of deft canine skill second to none,
a combination of economy,
energy and sheer artistry
whole lives are spent trying to achieve.

EXPERIMENTS

It's April 1943.

The air is warm and the inhabitants of this Northern world
are testing out the notion that Winter is past,
along with the edibility of pignuts,
ground elder and other less appetising items.

In fact, experiments are going on all over Europe:
in Warsaw, Den Hague, even Switzerland,
where a young chemist accidentally ingests traces
of a substance he's been working on for some time

that send him spinning through the streets of Basel
at such speeds he sprouts wings,
spends the day in the company of angels and demons
before coming back down.

Little does he know that when he's back on solid ground,
his research will have certain repercussions in years to come,
will beget experiments on survivors from Treblinka,
CIA men, the odd Vietcong volunteer,

sending many more into orbit,
until around the time those born in April 1943 come of age,
a substance demonised, it will go underground
enabling some to find God, others white rabbits,

or a warp and weave that's hard to leave.
And so my problem child, he writes years later.
*Conceived in time of darkness, led astray by those who sought sensation,
a footnote in history of which I am no longer proud.*

To which I want to reply, don't worry Dr Hoffman,
every experiment casts a shadow, but yours pales
beside many undertaken in those warm spring days.
But we get ahead of ourselves, as it's April 1943,

and when this young man wakes he must clear his head,
continue with his work – as work makes you free!
While across Europe the experiments continue:
at Birkenau where the good doctor pursues his interest in genetics

at Peenemünde and Porton Down, and London
where the church bells ring for the first time in three years,
and in Paris where Sartre discovers
there is no ultimate purpose in this world.

RUN

Come on Grandad,
you're old enough to know
what the sound of gunfire means

take your bag,
the roubles mother thrusts
into your hands,

father's whiskery blessing,
run as fast as you can
through incendiary streets

to Limburg's mill.
The chestnut mare
will be harnessed –

the cart ready – but hurry,
they won't wait long.
There's no time for tears,

can't you hear what's happening –
Come on Grandad, run.

369 WEST REGENT STREET

As the war approaches, he spins seventy-eights
in his room overlooking police headquarters,
spends his evenings reading up on the anatomical
niceties of the ear, nose and throat.

Lilah, his lavender, macaroon-loving aunt,
sits downstairs in her candle-lit parlour, a shawl
covering the cage of her cantankerous African grey,
and grips the damp tremulous hands of clients

around the scarred mahogany table, admiring
the pale seepage of their auras – viridian, rose,
indigo – as they wait for the dead to compete
with disembodied voices from radiograms.

First up, corporal Mackay lost on Messines ridge,
who's finally found his voice after twenty years
in no man's land, the words somehow squeezed
out of Lilah's distorted larynx as his widow

weeps by her side, followed by the Honourable
Hamish McFadden, subaltern in the Scots Guards
atomised near Amiens. Lastly, gravel-voiced
garrulous Tam Gordon from Cowcaddens,

who drowned in the mud near Langemark,
but has kept up a long-term communication
with his sister Belle, his voice distant and echoey
like a transatlantic telephone conversation.

Of little interest to her scientific young relative
on the second floor, who smiles as he draws and labels
neat diagrams of the speech and vocal tract, hums
to the hiss and groove of Beiderbecke's golden horn.

SELF-SUFFICIENCY

I'll know when it's time
to dig that trench
beneath the copper beech
at the field's edge,
shovel spoil into a hessian sack,
tie it to a branch
that overhangs
this shallow grave;
to scatter poppy, bluebell,
wild garlic into limestone,
leaf-mould and pale clay,
so when the end draws near
I can climb in and use
the remaining strength
of once powerful limbs
to tug the cord,
unseam the sack,
the effort causing me
to fall back as the rope swings,
soil covers me from head to toe,
such preparation
being at the heart of all things.

PRESSING

What better
than to fill wheelbarrows
with windfalls,

to wash and pulp them,
shovel them into
the barrel of the press;

to listen to the hiss and crackle
of compressed apple,
the creak of sodden oak –

feel the effort of iron
as the plate is screwed down
bit by bit –

see the sudden rush
of juice that spills
into saucepan and jug,

until every last drop
is squeezed out of it.
What better than

to gulp down great draughts
until your stomach
aches with it,

feel a step closer
to the shift of the season
on that peel-scuffed floor.

THE COMMISSION

Horse & Dog Trim
The property of G.W. Ricketts whose life was saved by the dog
by G. Stubbs

While at Longwood, he spends time sketching
and making notes about his subjects; at dinner

hears of Jamaican estates, the tan mongrel's
timely act, the bay hunter's skill at chase.

Later, out searching for a suitable prospect,
he places dog and horse as if communing

by a stand of oaks, looking down towards
house and lake – the distant line of low hills.

The piece, as always, is full of false starts –
proportion's elusive, the horse's neck causes problems;

and he's troubled there's no sense of the under-
lying story – the figure creeping through

the night – the knife, the shame – the purgatory
of picking cane beneath the overseer's brutal eyes.

WALNUTS

My mind ebbs and flows like the tide
– John Clare

On All Souls he slices away the green husks
that oxidise when exposed to air, stain his fingertips
as he soaks them in a pot of rainwater.

At first frost, stews them over a slow fire,
the pungent liquid (reeking of ditch and dyke)
reduced until it turns dark brown, strained

though a square of old sacking, stored until
the urge to write comes over him and words
surge through his wrist like sap in springtime

across thin sheets of birch-bark paper
detailing the habits of badger, dotterel, woodman,
mouldiwarp – a frenzy of loops, twists,

blotches, dashes that summon throstle, cowslip
and the rage of the blundering plough –
until drained of words, the need to empty

the head of images – the inkwell runs dry.

THE QUARRIES

supplied stone for the houses of merchants
and weavers, the churches and soaring mills

until these hillsides were riddled with workings,
tunnels through layers of limestone and clay,

shafts along fissures scoured by melt-waters,
their wave-worn ceilings scalloped with shells.

Three centuries of subterranean endeavour,
till stone fell from favour, railways brought brick.

Then dormant, dripping places, rubbish tips
and secret storage spaces explored by boys

with torches and balls of string who searched
for the sleepers by the underground lake,

some returning with tales of strange sightings,
others, who limped home, exhausted and pale.

DEEPDALE BECK

This is a land where what you see
is only part of what there is.

Take this beck:
in winter the weight
of water from moor and fell
masks all sense of it.

Look at it now, a series
of shallow pools, a swirl of parched limestone

punctuated by springs that bubble
up from the depths,

plugs through which
everything disappears
only to resurface downstream.

Walking here reminds you
of how sight favours surfaces,
what lies beneath skin.

Step out of sunlight into this
shadow landscape – warmth
into subterranean chill –
the world
will never look the same again.

FIRST KILL

One moment loping down
through the sap-green
world of the wooded scarp,
the next, she's gone.
I wait, whistle: nothing
but peevish jackdaws,
the wood's quiet exhalation.
Back through the trees
she's pinned down a buck,
legs thrashing as she tears
at its ragged throat,
struggles to finish it off.
I kick her away, snatch up
a beech-stave and strike,
the blow instinctively held back,
glancing off antler and out-
stretched neck; then again,
and again, finding a rhythm,
feeling the shock of bough
on muscle and bone,
the shudder of the beast's body,
until it lies sprawled
in a crush of ramson-flowers,
the dog beside it, vomiting bile
and blood-soaked mercury,
in need of oxygen, before
we can head up towards the light.

LUNGWORT

Despite his mistrust of sympathetic magic
and the doctrine of signatures,

Keats picked the speckled leaves
and arterial blooms of Pulmonaria

that grew so freely on the fringes of the heath,
to make a bitter infusion, a tea

sweetened with honey to soothe
his ravaged throat, while he sat

and dreamed of travelling through
realms of gold, the breathless south.

THE LIFT

Even without his hearing-aid,
he catches the swirl of cornets
through the open window,

the sound of voices as a pleasure-
steamer passes through the lock,
prompting memories of the night

sixty years back they shifted
the hospital piano into the lift,
spent the evening travelling up

and down between the wards,
singing, playing their hearts out,
fortified by youthful exuberance,

by beer and the knowledge
that hostilities had finally ended.
Until the supervisor was forced

to come and calm his raucous
Housemen, leaving many a patient
delusional from morphine or pain,

bereft of the strains of *Basin Street*
and *Ain't Misbehavin'* that rose
and fell in the close city night.

APPLE BANDIT

All year he's a rumour,
a word half-forgotten
in the dark hemisphere of the brain,
dormant, in part dream,
the thermostat of his heart set low
until the swifts have gone
and orchards exude an invisible ripeness.
Then night after night
in the dew of late summer darkness
he takes shape again,
a shadow fleshed out
by the fluids of galaxies
seeping across the depths
of the night sky.
Undeterred by piss or picket fence
he comes up and over the wall
craving windfalls,
the ferment and scent of spiked apple,
unaware that I too am out,
drawn by the hiss of burning stars.
Wild-nosed, incautious,
he glows as he gorges, fattening to a taper,
to a tallow flaring in the darkness,
the bulk of his body,
the shape and stripe of his otherness
edging blindly closer
until the flat crunch of his jaws
is so close I flinch,
sudden movement that sends him
up and over pale drystone,
to lie low until I'm weary of waiting,
a half-forgotten shape
in the dark hemisphere of his brain.

CAMELLIA

Come April
in a world waking
from drabness

look at me says
the Camellia,
aren't my scarlet

blooms a reminder
of what you've
been missing?

Forget insipid
cherry blossom,
the cheap perfume

of bluebells –
scent is so over-rated
adore only me.

CLEARING PARK WOOD

This numb green summer morning we process
an ash so keen to soak up lakeside light
it failed to send out tap-roots front and back,
weakening its grip on heavy bankside clay.
It could be a moral tale about greed, desire,
how the mighty fall – the mind skims such thoughts
as we save it from water's swift decomposition.
Working with rope and saw, we lop boughs
from its part-submerged form circled by damselflies
and dreamy carp. A suicidal bullfinch
fails to gauge the mood as each branch
is winched up the bank. And so it disappears,
leaving twisted root-ball, a memory, space vacated.

CRANES FLYING

My spade unearths
a piece of porcelain
this cool morning:

a bamboo thicket,
a pair of doves
flying over an island

covered in peach
and flowering plum.
Somewhere in the soil

must lie a pavilion
on a desolate mountainside –
stove and simple bed,

a desk fashioned
from Huanghuali wood
at which a scholar

inscribes the tale of two lovers
thwarted by caste,
family, convention –

sipping wine as he works,
pondering isolation,
exile, failure,

his observations recorded
in pithy lyrics
scribbled on margins

of the page, before
slipping into other realms
where he dreams

of cranes flying
across the face of a blood moon,
a lake choked

with lotus flowers,
two figures hurrying
across a bridge.

Alas, I get ahead of myself,
my spade turns up nothing
but pipe-stems, shells

fragments of the material world.
Ah, there is always
so much digging to do.

MAKING

Flat-chiselling
the fourth leg of a chair
I become impatient
with calipers,
a blade that takes off
too much or too little,
wanting it to be
the same smooth diameter
as the other three,
so step away
from the treadle,
trying to remember
Ruskin's words
on imperfection
and the ends of craft,
that this is a process
of muscle and bone
and unevenness,
(the faint line
of a spoke-shave,
marks of lifted grain)
is nothing
to be ashamed of,
but show how it is
to work under
a turf-smoked roof
that moves to the rhythm
of creaking lathes.

THRIFT STREET ILLUSIONIST

Slipping out of the shadows
he greets me like some long lost friend.

Have you a penny? he asks,
words issued between blackened stumps.

I give him a pound, which he palms
and asks me to call.

Says tails before I can, hands it back,
laughs. I don't drink, he says,

even though there's a faint smell
of something, is it brimstone or memory

on his breath? I pass him the coin again,
he palms it, but this time it's heads.

Tails, he says, weathered cheeks creasing
into a crooked smile –

and you believed me, like the guy
on the corner whose bottle disappeared

when I snapped my fingers –
and how mad was he?

I don't drink he says, as night hurries past
and shifts before my eyes into a child

on his way to school, to a raw recruit,
to a mass of knuckled pain – then back

to this wiry, grey-haired figure with brown
and twinkling eyes. I pass him the coin.

I don't drink, he says, mutters tails,
always tails, shuffles away into the night.

BLACK AND WHITE NIGHT

Do not wait up for me this evening
– Gérard de Nerval

Was it drink, despair or your double
that led you through icy streets
till, footsore, half-frozen,
you fetched-up at the door of a doss-house
in an alley off le Chatelet?

When the door wouldn't open,
was it something the raven said,
sinister bird with a burned black eye,
that led you to tie your rope
to the bars of the ventilation grille?

Did you hear death's trumpet blow
as you hung in the shadows,
sirens singing to you
as you swung in the biting cold?

LATE AFTERNOON, BREE STREET

Three road-sweepers in orange tops
rake (eucalyptus?) leaves
from the lip of a storm-drain –

a drunk waves a plastic coffee-cup
at the window of a taxi,
weaves past a *Big Issue* seller

who works his way down a line of cars
(without much luck).
A parking attendant

(unofficial, I suspect)
in an official-looking fluorescent bib,
covers the ground like a cheetah

when he clocks a Japanese tourist
backing into a parking bay
(badly, it must be said)

as a pair of scavengers
with rucksacks and gloves
work the bins outside TJ's warehouse.

But who's the guy in a green tabard
scanning the street from the door
of the Lord's Place?

Those two lurking by the entrance
to Boggie's Bock?
Surely not bouncers at this time of day? –

although the winter light's thickening
and voices spill from the bar
below.

And who's the woman
stationed by the lights
as a boy skateboards through a red

barely missing a taxi
as it pulls in outside the hotel –
or the youth who shadows me

when I step out
to get a breath of wood-smoke and dust,
to watch the sky bleed

through pink to rust as the sun goes down
over Table Mountain.

GLADSTONE FELLS A TREE

Back from Westminster
after another officeless year,
out walking in the park
he falls in with his foresters
who are about to fell an ash.
Hefting an axe, one blow
is all it takes to see that
here is a means to expend
excess energy, to balance hand
with a head that's filled with Homer
and restless political schemes.
Hooked by the knuckle-shock of it,
he barely listens as bird's mouth
and kerf are explained,
is miles away, moving into
a darker area of the brain
where he'll find solace,
the strength to see him through
successive stormy ministries,
satisfaction incomplete
until, stiff, sweaty, he watches
the ash come crashing down.

ALL SOULS IN SEVASTOPOL STREET

I am standing on the threshold of another trembling world
– Bobby Sands

Moments later, a cab arrives and out step a young couple.
He, holding a camera while she crosses the road,
poses beneath the poet's mural in plain view of the cctv,

oblivious to the hum of a helicopter over Andersonstown.
Smiles. They swap, kiss in mid-street as the cabby
drums his fingers, then off to the tour's next port of call.

Seconds later, another draws up. All day they come,
on into dusk, but less solid as midnight approaches,
the figures slipping out of them spectral: fellow prisoners,

priests, volunteers from nearby murals, to spit, exchange words
over ideology, feuds, darkness of conscience, old arguments,
the fag-ends of which still glow in death's gutter.

Each group moves to stand beneath the smiling face – click,
the image captured by the afterlife's official photographer.
Some wincing, others ducking as rockets hiss overhead,

but all ignoring the quiet urgency of the lost foot patrol
duck-footing it through shadows on the far side of the street.
The faces of this noiseless gathering lit by the torches

of passing revellers, who fail to notice this crack in the year's
descent into darkness. Until the man himself, no longer skeletal,
steps down to share a smoke among the decommissioned

and disparate dead, like a host among his guests, shaking hands,
making jokes, calming disputes, till dawn's light touches the flags
on the roof of the Divis flats, and all evaporates.

TWO MINUTES AND THIRTY-SEVEN SECONDS

New York, 1916. Suspended mid-air over
a subway excavation, hanging by his feet from a hook

head full of blood, the man they call Houdini
frozen in the process of a moment.

A group of labourers look on from nearby scaffolding,
some tight-lipped towards the camera, others

spellbound as he sways a hundred and eighty feet
above the street like a giant pendulum in the breeze,

one who stands by the rail and smiles, who sees
that anything is possible in this land of the free.

At first, it's the breathless anarchy of such an act that moves me,
the composition of hanged man and winter bough;

then the scene's grainy realism: the foreman's face
pinched with impatience at these onlookers, Poles, Germans,

economic migrants who too are in the act of escaping.
But inevitably it's the figure at the photograph's heart

swinging high above these upturned faces the eye is drawn to,
the recognition of all those cuffs and chains,

the quiet exhilaration of knowing that at any moment
he might slip and plunge into the deep pit below.

ARCHAEOLOGY

Pheasants and foraging owls
slip through the layers of fissured chalk
into the still-pool of sleep past fire-lit faces,
figures slipping away into the darkness,
surfacing to wood-smoke and starlight
before the earth opens again.
You lie in the ring-ditch listening,
spinning through double-light, falling
faster and faster until flesh, sinew and bone
are stripped away. You are transformed,
a coil of white-hot steel that drills down
through the strata of solidified time
into a place that is no place you can
imagine or have reached before.

BARK

Just off the white track,
a ring of beech around a barrow,
towering trees
whose roots reach down
to cradle mound and chamber
in their chalky grasp,
their silvered bark
as pocked and fissured
as the weathered sarsens
that guard the entrance
to the world beyond.
The trunk of each
mapped with scars:
names, dates, symbols,
crude alphabets cut by blade
or broken glass
celebrating love and loss –
shelter taken from sun or squall.
Some small record
of how it is to be
amidst these towering trees –
to slip beyond the realm of wood
and lichened stone, let
this gathering place
sink into skin and bone.

TOMB

As the settlement grows, does the shaman
see a sign while travelling in the spirit world,
in a heart-shaped leaf, two hawks sparring
or the entrails of a sacrificial beast and say
build here – as elevation and under-surge
make this the perfect gathering place high
above the dangers of the wooded plain?

Do they raise this oval mound, this vessel
of chalk, earth and oak, by forcing slaves
to drag sarsens up these punishing slopes,
because they're driven by the need to bury
sacred bones, to beg the reluctant sun to rise –
to come and warm their shivering bodies
and souls, beneath this expanse of pale sky?

THAT SPRING

Resolved to confront followers of the old ways,
I set out across forest and flatland reaching the ridge
where they worshipped at sunset on the third day.

Drawing near in growing darkness, I listened
to their songs – what I took to be charms chanted
by naked figures leaping over a bed of low flames.

Stepping forward into the firelight, I held up
my cedar cross, preached about the danger of idolatry –
how *He* welcomes sinners back into the fold.

Some seconds they stood as if terrified, unable
to withstand the power of my text, made crude signs,
cried out then slipped away leaving *Him* victorious,

and me to destroy all evidence of their practices,
to sprinkle holy water over the standing stones,
bury a shard of a saint's thighbone as the sun rose.

A TRAVELLER'S TALE

At dusk-fall I led my mare off the old white track
tethered her between two weathered stones
lit a fire and listened to the wind –
my horse whickering at night's unfamiliar sounds –
lay a coin at my feet, just in case.

Cushioned by the mound I fell into feverish dream
felt heat and flame, a hammer beating out iron;
through sparks and smoke saw a shadowy figure,
black-hewed, strong as oak
shaping a shoe on the horn of his anvil.

When I woke in the shivering dawn and shook off
night's strange freight, the silver was gone,
my mare reshod.
This is how it is, a tale told over,
embellished, refined, till it's nothing less than fact.

IMPROVEMENTS

Just weeks back from the warm south,
I am riding along the ridge barely seeing
the cornflowers, poppies, soaring kites,
so full are my thoughts of columns, arches,
the wonder of Rome's sprawling streets.

When my horse shies at some invisible
danger in the depths of a hawthorn hedge,
I lead her off the track through a thicket
hung with strips of faded cloth, emerge
at the entrance of a plough-bitten barrow.

The view's sublime. Instinct tells me
this ruined tomb's the place to start –
restore the stones, plant a ring of beeches –
a sacred grove for philosophers to come
and contemplate priests in flowing robes.

DEFIXIONES

Temple of Mercury, Uley, AD 276

Tools laid out on the low bench,
he awaits his first customer,
warming his hands before the fire,

wonders not for the first time
how he wound up here
in this edge-land above the estuary.

How he who dreamt of writing poems
to match those of his Roman masters
ever sank so low as to survive

on the back of superstition,
scratching spells onto squares of lead
in a shelter by the temple gate.

Maledictions to empower the mad,
the desperate and the needy,
paid for in coin or kind.

Punish him Father, for putting
the eye on my few cows.
Curse Matua who covets my husband,

consume her stinking blood.
Simple formulas he refines, expands,
inscribes on curse-tablets,

binds and pierces with bronze pins,
casts into a pit in the woods below
as he intones the ritual words

Bescu

   Bazagra

      Berebescu

THE ORIGIN OF AN IDEA

Prone he lay, chin uppermost, as though in pain…
Hyperion

Fascinated by Cibber's *Melancholy*
sprawled across Bedlam's gated arch,

young Keats composes his face to match
the statue's mournful vacancy, keeping

a keen eye on the movement of the wind,
of course; comparing it with those seen

in street or court, lips moving silently,
their moon-shot eyes staring at invisible

figures of the air, or passing through
the institution's gates to seek admission

for relatives or themselves. Practices
that pursue him back to evening's darkened

parlour, where he's loath to look in the fly-
blown glass for fear of what he might see.

IN TRANSLATION

I imagine some footsore ethnographer
heading up through peach orchards
to a remote village on the fringes of the Huishan forest.
An earnest fellow equipped with bags,

specimen jars, a crumpled pocketbook
for noting down the words of a wizened old woman
through the lens of an interpreter;
a famous healer who's grinding

the knuckle-bones of a muntjac
between flat stones, the resulting powder
moistened with plum-blossom honey,
smeared on strips of cloth to be bound round knees,

ankles, calves, to ease fatigue, soothe
inflammation after a long day in the fields.
As she hawks into the fire-pit I imagine
his eyes being drawn to the rows of jars

on shelves containing what look like
songbirds, organs, reptiles
suspended in rose-coloured fluids –
at pieces of purple bark nailed to a beam,

a string of desiccated ears, monkeys he hopes,
that seem to twitch and home in
on the dry hinge of the old woman's tongue
every time she speaks.

LAMMAS LOAVES

Yeast froths as you busy yourself with brush and ball,
full of the hum of sounding words
that bubble up from your depths
as the cool sift of flour grains my palm map.

Up, you demand, as I work in oil and water, *up*;
hands echoing my movements,
heeling and slapping the dough, until a passing tractor,
the solitary traffic of a village deserted by summer

drags you away in a whirl of breathless naming –
the word expanded, tested through shifts
of volume and intonation, till the bowl is placed
on the lip of the worm-bored sill.

Back you come, your restless prepositions
pulling us out into rising day, to tug at raspberry canes,
runner beans – further still, out into the sea
of husked wheat, whose waves harden

into a sickled curve, where you stumble,
bruising knees on cracked earth, bewildered
by the gulf between us, the weighted sky;
repeating the sound of pain,

until safe on my shoulders
we soak up homeward textures, ripening blackberries,
the movement of meadow ewes.
Absorbing details on the edge of the known world

until, back in the kitchen, the mixture has risen,
its surface as pitted as the harvest moon,
and you fall asleep, leaving me to shape the loaves,
to doze while they prove in warm sunlight.

FIVE MINUTES

cook says, making tea, words Paul echoes,
hands stiff from peeling potato and swede.

Looking at his watch he finds little in its face
to tell him what five minutes might be,

to help him understand this foreign tongue
of time to which no one can supply the key.

Besides, people tell him what to do
and when to do it. Time's being told to get up,

to go, to put your boots on, is something
that disappears when you are having fun,

but bears little relation to this disc ticking
on his wrist. Five minutes: easily forgotten

as a dog yelps by the door, amidst the clatter
of pans, the scuff of boots across the floor.

THE FLOW

We're making an apple-ladder
from a slender ash
shouldered to this workshop,
where afternoon slips away
to the thud of yew on dented steel,

working with froe and maul,
a side-axe so sharp
it could cut through light,
a dialogue with shape and sap
that leaves human residues far below.

How beautifully bark strips,
so moist and green,
how tough to work
these knotted whorls, to lose
such clarity as darkness falls.

TASTING NOTES

The first materialised in a cellar near Belfort.
A huge brute of a thing that padded around after the patronne,
its coat as dark and dense as the wine
that was tannin-heavy, heady even.

A rescue dog from a Paris flat, its eyes were fathomless, blank,
as if the change of latitude was still fermenting
quietly in its soul, and like the wine needed time
and warmth to bring out its true nature.

The second barking ferociously, showing a fine set of teeth
when we pulled into the domaine above Cordes,
turned out to be a comedian, an acrobat
performing turns on an old wicker chair,

every bit as mercurial as the perfumed Gaillac
that tasted of sweet pepper and sunshine,
had us reaching for our wallets
as we moved out of the fierce afternoon light.

The last in a dusty yard near Blois took no notice when we arrived.
Paralysed it lay pooled in gloom beneath the cherry tree,
an omen we chose to ignore, keen
to be out of the sun and into the shadowy cave beyond.

The wine we sampled was a compulsive yet corrosive red
which after one glass too many had the effect
of deadening limbs, tongue, judgement –
all appetite for the long road ahead.

SAFETY IN NUMBERS

Across the table Razak,
wide-eyed, giggling, four days
after hospitalising his mother.

    Shaken by the seep
of corrosive fragments,
I tempt him

with tight little grids
of numbers across a neutral page,
and to my surprise

he falls in with it.
Brutal work this, keeping him
from the sump of race and family.

It is my uncles he begins
(numbers drifting in
and out of focus),

they stay and what they say
you know... the pen
knife-like in his fist.

As he works I am struck
by the sheer futility of the task,
but also by how such futility

brings a curious sense of relief.
Don't turn your back on him
they say, but how could I?

seeing him tapping out residuals
knuckling them,
finding safety in numbers

till the session's end.

TRAVELLER'S TALES

Neither the ramblings of an aged relative
or tales told in passing taverns
prepared me for that first sight of it.

Delirious with hunger and the effects of sun,
felled by a tuft of sea-pinks,
I lay gazing down past gull-ledges

at the beaten surface of the sea below,
panicked by the heave and maw of it,
finding no words to describe

horizon or the motion of wind and tide,
but content to absorb it
through every pore in my aching body;

half-remembered stories giving shape
to the haunting cries
of what I took to be seal-people,

fish-tailed beings, sea-serpents
that I worked into tales intricate enough
to beguile my credulous, land-locked brethren

who lived way back over mountain, marsh
and moor, and knew nothing of black rocks,
the sea's spume and yaw.

AT PORT NA BA

The real history of consciousness starts with one's first lie

– Joseph Brodsky

As black cows cross the crescent of white sand
this cool summer morning, shags dive,
the Small Isles rise from a cloud-dark sea,
I recall reading of Finn, Lord of the Fianna
by long forgotten torchlight, the heroic past
colliding with the present when mother
came to check my light was off. How I hid
quiet laughter welling up inside, the book
beneath my covers, by pointing at the map
above the bed, these same Isles, Muck, Eigg
and Rum displayed there, names strangely
compelling to a boy like me who'd rarely
been north of the Clyde, but drifted through
Hebridean channels each night and far out to sea.

DOG AND FOX

Working the hedgerow,
she marks a fox
out between the rows
of frosted beets,
so intent on vole
or field-mouse
it hears nothing,
until she accelerates
across frozen soil.

Pigeons scatter,
fieldfares, a single
raw crow curses
as they clear the fence,
hurtle down through
the hazel coppice
between stump
and dormant stool.
I wait by the gate

until back she comes
loll-tongued,
limping slightly,
and on we go.
Rock-hard of rut
and track-ice, the earth
has tightened up again,
is muscle-tense
against the cold.

ROOF

After a century's worth of weather
the roof of this hilltop house
is removed slate by cracked slate,
boots and hammers, dust, rubble,
as four tons of lichened stone
and skims of brittle and torching
are hacked off to disclose
the secret paperwork of wasps.
Stripped of cussom, bachelor, short-cock,
the house breathes, settles old bones
and dreams of renewal, the power
of pitch and pendle to withstand
another century of wind and rain,
and prays for an august drought,
its skull open to the unfelted sky.

10 CAVENDISH CRESCENT

Landscape with drover, Jan Asselyn

Up early unable to sleep he shuffles
into the study, a stiffness in his bones,
turns to the landscape above his desk.

The room still starved of light,
little is visible beyond the bull's pale horns,
the gleam of its bony flanks.

So he sits and listens to the clock ticking,
hooves clattering over the cobbles outside
until the day grows bright enough

for the canvas to become suffused with light –
trees, cliff, drover in his tattered clothes
to be touched by the sun rising over the Campagna

somewhere to the south of Rome.
Ah, the south. He feels the heat of it
on his face and hands, smells dust, dung

and crushed thyme as he sips his coffee,
wonders again what the bull is looking at,
where time and life have gone.

A SINGLE MALT

Some months after the conflict started,
I was scabbing for firewood in the backroom
of what was the Carpenter's Arms.

Scarfed against the smell but retching still,
I stumbled across a dust-covered bottle
buried at the back of a broken shelf.

Uncorked, cool in my hand, the heat
of that first nip was sweet, slightly smoky –
Bruichladdich, Laphroaig, Lagavulin?

I wasn't sure, but the taste of it conjured
sitting with Terry and Uncle Les
the day after the signing of the *Riga Accord*;

five-fifteen of a Saturday,
place packed with regulars picking over
Forest Green's latest loss – light, heat

the smell of slopped bitter and hops,
from the back bar a voice on the radio
going on about a build-up of troop movements

on the Polish border, Les turning to us
and saying *storm in a teacup*
with all his placid avuncular certainty.

ACKNOWLEDGEMENTS

Versions of some of these poems have appeared in the pamphlets *The Last Walking Stick Factory* (Happenstance), *In Bedlam's Wood* (Templar), and the following magazines and anthologies:

Interpreter's House, Agenda, Dreamcatcher, Gutter, Other Poetry, Warwick Review, Smiths Knoll, Raceme, The High Window, The Frogmore Papers, Mixed Borders, Battered Moons Anthology, Buzzwords, The Emma Press Animal Anthology, The Echoing Gallery, The Holburne Museum Anthology. 'Cranes Flying' won the 2018 GWN prize.

Thanks to the judge of the 2018 Beverly Prize, Dr Bruce Meyer, to my editor Alex Wylie and to all at Eyewear. Also thanks to Jane Draycott and Philip Gross for their helpful comments.

Lightning Source UK Ltd.
Milton Keynes UK
UKHW040757111220
374935UK00004B/25